TRANSFORMING FACILITIES INTO COMMUNITIES

Anthony Brewer

TRANSFORMING FACILITIES INTO COMMUNITIES

TRANSFORMING FACILITIES INTO COMMUNITIES

Anthony Brewer

ISBN: 9781304803993   (Paperback)

Library of Congress Control Number: 2021908737

Cover design and Illustrations by BizVizionary.

Printed by Lulu, Inc., in the United States of America.

First printing edition 2021.

TRANSFORMING FACILITIES INTO COMMUNITIES

Anthony Brewer

ISBN: 9781304803993   (Paperback)

Library of Congress Control Number: 2021908737

Cover design and Illustrations by BizVizionary.

Printed by Lulu, Inc., in the United States of America.

First printing edition 2021.

" The Power of community to create health is far greater than any physician, clinic, or hospital."

- Mark Hyman
American Physician

TABLE OF CONTENTS

FRONT MATTER

BACK MATTER

DEDICATION

This book is dedicated to all the residents I have had the privilege to serve.

ACKNOWLEDGMENTS

I want to acknowledge those who contributed their knowledge and expertise to the development of this manuscript, including Dawn Cass, Dawn Kollasch, Esther Sperling, Heather Jordan, Karen Iversen, Kirk Heng, Shelli Dannenberg, and Tyson Dukes.

I wish to thank Jenny Wahl-Rupp and Kyle Wray who provided detailed and constructive feedback and recommendations on early drafts. I also want to thank one of my best friends, Paul Hittner, for designing the cover of this book and inspiring me to become an author.

I am immensely grateful for Chris Wolf and Mike Hocking. These two incredible nursing home administrators encouraged me to pursue this path and imparted me with a fraction of their wisdom and experience.

Finally, I want to thank my mother, Nikki, for never giving up on me and always pushing me to be the best version of myself that I can be. She is the strongest women I know and my hero.

INTRODUCTION

Sterile, institutional, depressing, weird smelling, low energy. These are words that many people associate with the term nursing home. When I hear the word facility, these are the terms that come to mind. In contrast, community evokes a sense of togetherness, warmth, and closeness. To transform a facility into a community is to promote an environment where residents thrive and staff are empowered. Happy residents result in fewer grievances, positive word of mouth, and better survey outcomes. Happy employees lead to lower turnover, less money spent on recruiting and training staff, reduction in overtime and agency expenses, and a higher quality of care given to our residents because of the bonus of familiarity.

I have boiled this recipe for success down to 3 Core Values that will guide you through this transformation. Although these values apply to virtually any industry or workplace, this work will be presented through the lens of a lifelong healthcare worker. I have included several Healthcare Hacks that can easily be implemented to support the 3 Core Values and aid you as you take the necessary steps to transform your facility into a community.

My experience with nursing homes began when I was only 10 years old. My family assisted in placing our elderly neighbor, Jeanette, in a nursing home. Knowing that she did not have any close family, my father would often show up at her house with a pizza and a six pack of beer to watch baseball games. Jeanette was a permanent fixture during my elementary years and became like an extra grandmother.

Jeanette started having trouble keeping up with her house. My family assisted her in moving into an independent living apartment. Each time we would visit, we noticed that she was becoming increasingly confused. As a child I did not understand dementia. It became apparent that her living situation was no longer safe. My family then helped her make the difficult decision to move into a nursing home.

Although Jeanette was angry because she felt as if she was being locked up, we continued to visit her frequently in the nursing home as the dementia progressed. I continued to love Jeanette dearly but grew to loath these visits. The facility felt very cold and institutional. This experience gave me a negative impression of nursing homes. I never would have guessed that I would eventually become a nursing home administrator. Now I am on a mission to transform facilities into warm and welcoming communities.

Early in my caregiving career, I met a man we will call Doug and my experience with him is something I will never forget. Doug lived in a nursing home where I worked as a CNA. He was a very interesting man whose room was decorated in war medals and sports awards. It was my third day on the job and my first day training on Doug's hall. As I was assisting him at bedtime, he became very short of breath and stated he could not breathe. I rushed to get the nurse, but she did not seem to be concerned or have any sense of urgency.

Despite my insistence, she told me that Doug would act that way every night when being assisted to bed. Following the orders of my charge nurse, I went back to Doug's room and continued helping him get ready for bed. Doug continued with the same shortness of breath and this time stated that he was dying. What happened next haunts me to this very day. He looked me square in the eyes and bluntly stated, "This is all your fault." His eyes rolled back into his head and he went limp. I ran to notify the charge nurse, yet again, and despite her continued resistance I demanded that she come check on him immediately. The nurse then assessed him and acknowledged that he had indeed died.

I will never forget how poorly Doug was treated by this nurse. I witnessed this once incredibly influential man reduced to someone who had no dignity left and was afraid for his life. This experience drives me to make sure that every resident is treated as if it is their last day on Earth and like they are the only resident being caring for.

As I continued my journey in healthcare, from dietary assistant to administrator, my core values became much more defined and began to place themselves firmly in my mind. These values have grown even more since my early days and have guided me in my mission to destroy the negative stereotypes and reshape the attitudes and beliefs held by many.

Whether you are a new manager or an industry veteran, I welcome you in taking the first step in transforming your facility into a community.

1
DIGNITY

Dignity is defined as "the quality or state of being worthy, honored, or esteemed" (Merriam-Webster, 2021). Treating someone with dignity essentially means to treat someone as an individual with opinions, values, and desires equal to your own. This is a desire shared by all people. How do you want to be treated? How would you want your parents or grandparents treated? Remember these questions when making decisions that impact residents or staff.

When a person does not feel like they are being treated with dignity, it affects how they treat others. Caregivers often have a difficult time treating residents and their coworkers with dignity because they themselves do not feel as if they are being treated with respect. Many are employed by managers who view them as low skilled workers who are easily replaced. They often find themselves on the receiving end of a resident who is acting out as a result of their dementia or other health complication.

If a resident does not feel as though they are being treated with dignity by staff, it affects their ability to treat others with dignity. As a result, they might begin treating their caregivers as their servants or start displaying abusive behaviors towards other residents. The cycle continues.

Dignity must be exercised by every employee at every level of the organization so that it permeates through every level of care. Follow the Golden Rule. Treat staff the way you would want to be treated and empower them to treat the residents as they would like to be treated.

RESIDENT DIGNITY

Often, residents of nursing homes feel as if they are a burden to their family. They may feel as if they are of no use and have no value to society. When a resident no longer feels like they have value, they are less likely to socialize or participate in activities. This leads to a further sense of isolation and depression. These emotions may cause a resident to feel they are not worthy of living or receiving care. They might stop participating in therapy and have a functional decline. An example of how this affects them could be incontinence. They do not think they deserve help going to the bathroom, causing skin break down and furthering their belief that they have no value.

Because of the important role that dignity plays in a resident's mental and physical well-being, we must do everything to protect it. The Centers for Medicare and Medicaid Services (CMS) requires:

> A facility must treat each resident with respect and
> dignity and care for each resident in a manner and
> in an environment that promotes maintenance or
> enhancement of his or her quality of life,
> recognizing each resident's individuality. The
> facility must protect and promote the rights of the
> resident (Resident Rights, 2019).

Protecting a resident's dignity includes talking to them in a respectful and professional manner. When providing care, staff should explain the care and give the resident a chance to respond and to refuse (even if he or she cannot comprehend what is being explained.) A simple joke a care giver makes to lighten the mood or pal around with the resident could be considered disrespectful, undignified, or even abuse. Age-appropriate terms should always be always.

One of the most frequent examples I see of this type of disrespect is the term bib, which is a word that invokes the thought of an infant. The age appropriate, and more accurate, term would be "clothing protector." Pet names and terms of endearment should be avoided, and caregivers should call residents their given name (or a nickname that s/he prefers). Terms like grandma, grandpa, hun, sweetie, etc., although done with the purest of intentions, can be considered disrespectful or undignified.

I worked in a facility where we had a resident everyone called Sweetheart. This was a life-long nick name that originated in middle school. Despite this being what all her family had always called her, in order to preserve her dignity, we could not just assume it was okay for staff to call her this. Upon further interview, this was indeed her preferred nickname and was written into the care plan as such. This situation is not uncommon, and through resident interviews and proper care planning you can honor this resident's preferred name while still providing them the dignity of asking their preference and protecting the organization by documenting as such. As our industry experiences a generational and cultural shift, it will also be important to treat preferred gender pronouns in this same manner. Some states are already putting forward regulations addressing this topic.

In addition to the way we speak to our residents, the way we treat them is equally important. This means making sure we treat our residents in a way that makes them feel valued, not like a child or person who has outlived their usefulness. They should be treated as an adult, no matter the extent of their disabilities. If a staff member is styling a resident's hair, it should not be set in child-like pigtails but something that is age appropriate. Activities should also be age-appropriate, such as Happy Hour and casino outings, not children's games or movies aimed at children.

Any questions or concerns should be taken seriously, be addressed, and receive a response. To ensure this, you must have a strong grievance program with timely and documented follow through (Grievances, 2019). This does not always mean the resident will get the answer they want; but it shows you took their concern seriously and provided them an answer, rather than ignoring their concern or taking an extended period to respond.

Call lights should be answered timely so that the residents feel like the priority they truly are. Sometimes staff are busy and must prioritize based on the urgency of needs or requests. Most residents are very understanding and aware of this, however, the simple act of stopping in and explaining to them that another resident has a more urgent matter that needs attention. Giving them an estimated (and realistic) time that you will return to help them, versus waiting until you have the time to respond fully to that resident's need will give the resident an appreciation for importance of the work you do. It shows them that you take their calls for assistance seriously.

Healthcare Hack

Conduct random call light audits and give out prizes for the employee who answers the call light first!

Hand out a different level prize based on response times.

Call light response times should be constantly monitored through audits. When staff know administration is monitoring, they are more likely to ensure this is what is happening. Some call light systems can print reports that show how long it took for a call light to be answered. I am not a fan of these as they often include misleading information such as a call light being answered timely, but the staff member forgot to turn it off or a call light that was turned off quickly without responding to the resident's request.

I recommend auditing call light times by going into a resident's room, turning on the light, and waiting to see how long it takes to be answered. This will also give you a chance to visit with the residents while you wait to see how they are doing. If you find that residents are consistently having to wait, you will want to address this through your QAPI program.

Another way we preserve the dignity of our residents is by providing privacy with respect to their healthcare and personal lives (Resident Rights, 2019). Staff should have a private area for conducting shift reports where other residents cannot overhear. Residents should have a private place for phone calls and a designated area where they can personally visit or hold gatherings. Your community should also be able to accommodate residents with a private space for physical intimacy.

The most important thing you can do to protect resident dignity is ensure staff receive proper education and training. At times, dignity is not practiced by staff because they do not know any better or may be due to a lack of desire or compassion. The staff member calling their favorite resident Grandma or putting a resident in pig tails might love the resident to death and see nothing with the way they are addressing the resident. In their mind, they are being kind and compassionate. It is important to ensure you are providing continuous. Remind them to follow the Golden Rule and always take those extra few seconds to stop and think about what they are going to say, and how it could be perceived.

EMPLOYEE DIGNITY

When staff are treated with dignity, they feel empowered and have an increased sense of pride in their work. This results in better quality care for your residents, improved morale, and decreased workplace injuries. This leads to lower turnover rates and reduced recruiting costs. The residents will also benefit with improved continuity of care. Staff will learn their preferences and routines and residents will build closer relationships staff, often seeing them as family. There are several methods you can employ to promote employee dignity.
The best way to promote employee dignity is by making them feel like their work and skill is valued and appreciated.

It is necessary to have upfront, honest, and transparent conversations with your employees. It is an open dialog and a two-way street. This is the best way to show staff you value their opinions and concerns. Address any performance concerns timely and truthfully, and work with staff to provide solutions. Always keep an open-door policy so staff can speak with you and do not have to make an appointment. Solicit their input on what the problem might be and take advantage of the ideas they must fix it. Host frequent staff meetings to cover any new or relevant information or policy changes. Explain to them the reasons or regulations. Do not just dictate policy. Review survey outcomes with your staff, so they are aware of any deficiencies and get feedback on how to address these deficiencies. Involve them in the QAPI process. Have frequent staff huddles at shift changes to communicate information, do not just post a sign. These practices also help you to be continuously aware of any challenges they are facing.
It is important to build trust among the team. People want to know the truth. They want to feel that you value them enough to share the whole picture and be open with them. The more we, as leaders, open up to staff and have honest dialog with them, the more trust and respect they have for us. If staff trust you and see that you are addressing their concerns then they will follow your instructions, work harder, and be more comfortable and appreciative. This leads

to a better team environment. Employees need to feel their opinions matter. If there is an employee who is performing poorly and it is not addressed, other staff feel they can get away with the same behavior. It makes your employees think you do not value the hard work they are doing, and they will quit trying to perform to a higher standard. It is a vicious cycle that gets started if performance concerns are not quickly addressed. Always remember the old saying, "praise publicly and council privately" and be consistent in addressing concerns with all staff.

> ## Healthcare Hack
>
> Purchase some nice Thank You Cards to keep on hand.
>
> When you notice an employee going above and beyond write them a quick thank you note.
>
> Don't say anything to the employee and mail this to their home.

The second most important way to promote dignity with staff is by providing recognition; recognizing the hard-work they do every day. Employee recognition is important because most employees need to feel valued and part of the team. An employee that feels valued and appreciated will often perform better than one that does not. It makes the employee feel noticed and/or important in the organization. I have used employee of the month programs, resident voted awards, random gifts of their favorite soda or candy bars.

Not that a verbal "thank you" on the spot doesn't go a long way, but a hand-written letter, mailed to the employee's home address, takes your appreciation a step further. Anyone can say thank you in passing in the hall, but to take the time to sit down and write a personalized letter thanking them for their work, providing specific examples, and mailing to the employee's home, shows you took time out of your busy day and made a point to recognize them. Don't overdo it. Not only would this be extremely time consuming, but if all the employees are getting this level of recognition, it takes some of the specialness out of it. Reserve this for employees who truly stand out, have gone above and beyond, or even the employee who might be struggling and could use the morale boost.

Many companies use Employee of the Month, quarterly, or annual awards to recognize their employees to varying degrees of success. I have never particularly liked these awards because it always seems to offend someone who isn't awarded the recognition or spurs gossip regarding those who are. I am more in favor of offering Years of Service acknowledgments, educational advancement recognition, and attendance awards, because they are less arbitrary, and everyone has the opportunity to earn them.

These are excellent opportunities for the employee to receive public recognition and they will improve the employee's feelings of self-value and importance. Years of service pins are something to easily budget for. They can be awarded to staff for reaching tenure milestones to recognize their dedication and for them to show off their longevity with the company. You can use whatever milestones you like. Typically, I have used one year, three year, five year, and every five years thereafter.

You can also show appreciation and recognition to all staff within a given department. Almost every department and position in your community has a nationally recognized day or week of appreciation. Gift baskets, gift cards, etc. are a great way to recognize the important role of each department and position.

Healthcare Hack

Compile a list of all departments and positions within the organization and create a calendar of appreciation days so that you ensure you are recognizing all departments and not just the larger ones.

Be sure to include employees who might be a department of one such as Administrative Assistants or Social Service Directors.

Social media is a powerful tool. Posting achievements and milestones of your employees is something they can easily share with their friends and family. Always make sure that if you are using social media that you get the employee's permission before posting anything as some staff might not be comfortable with their information being posted online. Start by getting signed consents from all staff and compiling a spreadsheet of who is and is not okay with their information being posted on social media.

In addition to recognition from your supervisor, peer recognition is also a powerful tool that builds team cohesion and allows staff to build each other up. A recognition board is something I have used with success in every one of the communities I was responsible for.

The concept is simple. Suzie does something to help Tim; covers his shift when he has a sick child, picks him up from work when his car broke down, or steps in and helps him with an issue at work. Tim then fills out a small slip thanking Suzie for her help and it is posted for her colleagues, residents, and families to see. This practice encourages employees to shift their focus from the negative interactions to the numerous positive qualities in their peers. This makes for happier more productive employees and reduce employee conflicts.

Healthcare Hack

Decorate a bulletin board and provide staff cards that can be filled out and posted to recognize and show appreciation to employees

Be sure this is in located in an area that visible to staff, residents, and visitors.

Make sure to include instructions and encourage family and visitors to participate!

Another similar tool that has been used for employees to recognize one another are employee telegrams I called ours Spirit Grams keeping with the theme of the company. Essentially this was a signed telegram from one employee to another recognizing their peer. It would then be given to the employee (I always gave them their favorite candy bar or soda along with it) and a copy would become a permanent piece of their personnel file. I always explained it to my staff as a "reverse write-up." From time to time, it is necessary to document some sort of performance concern which would then become part of that employees file and would be reviewed during evaluations. But what about all the good things? Let's normalize capturing positive performance as it is just as valuable as negative performance.

No matter how much we love our job and are committed to our residents, we all have moments of frustration. Provide your employees a personal space to unwind and take a minute to collect themselves. This helps with care giver burnout and staff blowing up at their co-workers, or worse, residents. Provide them with a quality break room with personal space for their belongings and a microwave for their lunch or a quick snack. If you can provide snacks for them, even better, but at a minimum provide a toaster and some bread for toast and, of course, the most essential tool for an employee, coffee.

A comprehensive study of the relationship between pay and employee motivation has shown that compensation is not a strong motivating factor for employees (Judge et al, 2010). While this may be true, everyone wants to be paid what they are worth. If you are paying significantly less or offering substantially less in the way of benefits, pick-up bonuses, shift differentials, or other fringe benefits, than a competing facility, staff will feel under-appreciated or under-valued and leave for the competition. Make sure you are doing wage studies of your competition at least annually but in some instances, more frequently.

When promoting dignity among your staff, you will cultivate a sense of loyalty to you, the organization, and your residents. This results in lower turnover and increased employee performance. Again, follow the Golden Rule and treat staff the way you would want to be treated by your supervisor.

2

INDEPENDENCE

Going together with dignity is independence. Independence is another central desire all humans share. Think back to how or your parents let you do something on your own for the first time. Independence helps increase your self-value and self-esteem, which directly impacts, not only your mental well-being, but also your physical well-being.

Independence is a critical aspect of resident care. You will find the term used hundreds of times throughout the thousands of regulations you are tasked with ensuring. Independence gets to the very core of a resident's sense of well-being and self-worth.
As with your residents, or any human being for that matter, independence is also a crucial aspect for staff. Just like when your dad took off your training wheels for the first time, employees feel a sense of respect and trust when their employer give them independence in their job. This does not mean free reign or not being held accountable. This means giving team members the trust to complete assigned tasks, in their own way, so long as they deliver the quality service outcomes you expect.

As the old saying goes, "There is more than one way to skin a cat," the same is true with many tasks at work. One person might put dishes away from left to right while another person might put them away by dish type. So long as the dishes are put away in the same amount of time and in the correct places, there really is no right way. As your employees feel more independent, so will you. You will have built a mutual trust that will not require you to micromanage every aspect of every procedure. This will promote a culture in which your employees will be confident in their decision-making ability and will not feel compelled to check in with you for every minor decision they make. This will not only promote independence but will free up some of your time. You can then use this time to focus on additional ways to continue to improve your community.
As we delve more deeply into how we can promote independence with both our residents and staff, you will see why this core value will not only make your life easier as a manager, but also how it will empower both your residents and staff to achieve and sustain their highest potential.

17

RESIDENT INDEPENDENCE

Decline in functional mobility is something that, left to Mother Nature, is an inevitable part of the aging process. As we age, most of us will be faced with the reality that we are no longer able to do the things that we could when we were younger. For some of us this might come in the form of no longer being able to run a marathon or operate the latest piece of technology with ease. For others, it presents itself in the form of not being able to keep up with basic yard work that was once enjoyable, or the ability to drive safely. For some, a complete dependence on another person to even go to the bathroom.

This decline in ability and functionality, can be detrimental to a resident's independence as they begin to have difficulties completing tasks that they were once able to complete with ease. Because of this, it is important to consistently monitor all residents for any potential decline, especially those most at risk because of advanced age, or recent illness or accident. If a resident begins to demonstrate a decline, or there are signs that a decline may be imminent, it is critical to put interventions in place to prevent or minimize its effects.

Per CMS requirements:

> A resident with limited mobility (must) receives appropriate services, equipment, and assistance to maintain or improve mobility with the maximum practicable independence unless a reduction in mobility is demonstrably unavoidable (Mobility, 2019).

The two most effective tools that we can use to prevent or minimize a functional decline is through the utilization and optimization of Part B therapy services and an effective restorative program.

Generally, any resident who is not receiving skilled therapy should be on either a restorative program or be part of your Part B caseload. Part B therapy was implemented for LTC's back in the 1970's with the direct intent to prevent decline of residents in nursing homes. CMS had purported that over the course of a year it was reasonable to expect that residents would experience a natural decline and increase in falls if they did not receive a basic level of therapy intervention. With this in mind, Medicare beneficiaries were allotted a minimum amount of hours/dollars to provide the resident an opportunity to strengthen and enhance their capabilities with one of these three disciplines.

Physical Therapy (PT) specializes in strength building and improving a resident's ability to transfer, walk, and independently operate any assisted mobility devices such as wheelchairs or walkers. PT is most often associated with those who are experiencing neurological and musculoskeletal declines. Common examples of this includes new joint replacements, stroke, general debility, joint pain, and neurological diseases such as Parkinson's and ALS.

Occupational Therapy (OT) specializes in promoting a resident's ability to provide themselves with Activities of Daily Living (ADLs). This includes dressing and proper daily hygiene. Because most of these ADLs require the use of arms, OT specialize in upper extremities and works with residents who have had a recent shoulder replacement or are having issues with their elbows and wrists.

One of the most overlooked disciplines is Speech Therapy (SLP). Speech Therapy (SLP) is probably the most misunderstood discipline. Many think SLP focuses only on helping residents pronounce words, but there are much more specific neuro and muscular issues they deal with. SLP can be provided to residents having issues swallowing foods which prevents them from safely enjoying food without increased risk for choking or aspiration. SLP also helps residents improve overall communication by improving cognition speaking,

Part B should be provided to LTC residents who are experiencing a decline, or who would be expected to decline as a result of a recent fall or illness. It is common for LTC residents to experience 2-4 instances/events per year in which they would benefit from these services. Part B services can also benefit new residents who are admitting due to a recent decline or illness but do not qualify to receive any skilled services.

Continuous training should be provided to staff to reinforce the expectation that if they see something that seems out of the ordinary, they need to report it to leadership to ensure therapy can intervene and decrease risks of falls/accidents. If you a catch decline quick enough then many residents avoid potential accidents, many of which end up being reportable. Families will be happy because their loved one is not having falls/accidents, which will save you many unpleasant phone calls. If your residents are not declining, they can stay as independent as possible, and your nursing staff aren't lifting as much. This way, you are cutting down on potential work comp injuries, result in happier staff and happier residents. The only way therapy can continue to see someone under Part B to maintain current function is when the patient has a progressive disease, and it takes the skill of a therapist to maintain their condition.

Unlike Part B therapies, Restorative Programs are designed to help the resident maintain their current functional status rather than to improve. Failure to ensure that a resident has an individualized restorative program that sets maintenance goals that are designed to prevent a decline in functional capability can result in weakening and deterioration resulting in a loss of independence.

Families want to know their loved one is going to continue to get exercise after therapy is done, as many are under the misconception that once discharged from that they will decline. Ensure that the resident and/or family are aware that current Medicare guidelines do not permit therapy to continue seeing someone to "maintain" their condition and that steps will be taken to ensure their current level of function. Make sure to highlight the fact that if there is a decline in the future, they can be picked up on

Part B therapy again. Families want to know their loved ones are not going to be forgotten about in the facility.

Transition from Part B to Restorative should be a team effort. When a therapist deems a patient no longer needs the skill of a therapist to provide services it is then transferred to a Restorative Program. Restorative nursing programs can happen simultaneously with therapy as long as they are not duplicating services. An example of this would be a situation in which an Occupational Therapist determines they no longer have to work on dressing with the patient so you would set up a restorative program to maintain that resident's ability to dress themselves. While Restorative is maintaining this function, the OT department can work on other goals such as grooming. Every patient discharged from therapy should have a Restorative Program.

A strong restorative will have 1-3 people (depending on size of facility) dedicated to restorative all day. The dedicated staff also need to be leaders in educating nursing staff to document and note appropriate time spent with a person when assisting in a Restorative Program. A dedicated Restorative Aide may spend all day doing strength exercises or walking programs, but they will need help from CNAs to also document dressing programs, other walks, etc. A Restorative Aide needs to be strong a leader! As mentioned above, residents on two or more programs can help increase daily reimbursement rate for residents on Medicaid.

Another way to protect resident independence is by ensuring that they can continue making their own choices and decisions. According to CMS:

> "The resident has the right to, and the facility must promote and facilitate, resident self-determination through support of resident choice… (Self Determination, 2019).

One powerful tool that you can use to accomplish this is the community's dining program. Meals are usually the highlight of the residents' day because it is an opportunity to gather with their peers, socialize, and receive good food. Not only do the meals have to be good, but like everyone, your residents crave variety and options. Remember how independent you felt when your parents took you to a restaurant and let you pick out the table you ate at? How about the first time they allowed you to tell the waiter your order instead of ordering for you?

Promoting independence in your dining program means that you must involve and know your residents. This requires meeting with your residents often and finding out their likes and dislikes. Although you will never please all of your residents all of the time, if you can please the majority with your standard menu and provide enough alternatives, you can make sure that everyone has an option that they enjoy and have some say in. It is important to make sure you are doing this, not just with breakfast, lunch, and dinner, but with snack options as well.

In corporate or larger LTC communities it is common for an outside company or food vendor to provide you with menus developed to ensure they are meeting all nutritional and food safety guidelines. Although there are some benefits to this practice, it is important to remember that the menu isn't written in stone. They do not know your residents, but you do. Any menu changes must be reviewed and signed by a Registered Dietitian prior to being implemented. But you should involve the residents and tailor the menu to reflect the needs and preferences of your community.

I have found that the best way to give residents a choice in their menu is to have a monthly food council meeting. The dietary manager meets with the residents to visit and discuss the quality of the food or dining services, review any upcoming events or policy changes, and review next month's menu and adjust as necessary.

One community that I was involved with introduced "Resident Choice Fridays" into their dining program. At the end of each food council meeting, the dietary manager would place the names of any residents who attended into a chef's hat and would then draw one name for each Friday in the following month. The winners would then get to choose what was for dinner that day. More residents started attending food counsel in hopes of winning, and quickly realized the benefits of being involved.

This community ended up having the food counsel with the highest percentage of resident attendance as well as the highest dining satisfaction scores for dining of any community I was a part of.

Although anecdotal, a consistent trend I have noticed in every single resident satisfaction survey I have reviewed is that 100% of the time communities that had a food counsel outperformed those without and the higher the percentage of resident participation the higher the score.

Another community program that is used to promote resident choice is the community's Activity Program. According to CMS:
The facility must provide…an ongoing [activity] program to support residents in their choice of activities… [and encourage] … independence… (Activities, 2019).

Healthcare Hack
Have the dietary manager start a community dining counsel. Start small with a group of 5-7 residents and go from there.
Recruit the resident least satisfied with the food and turn them into your biggest cheerleader!

Activity programs should offer residents the opportunity to be productive and social, not merely entertained. While BINGO is entertaining for many residents and a staple in most nursing facilities, it is important to set your community apart from the rest by taking time to get to know your residents on a more personal level. This allows you to develop a more specialized and targeted activity program that increases social interactions and elevates the mood of your residents, many of whom are suffering from depression and isolation.

Activities such as men's club, book club, or garden club focus on both individual interests and bring residents together to share ideas and stories. Resident peer groups are more individualized because they are designed for those who belong to a specific demographic or share a similar interest or hobby. This encourages residents to contribute, and take pride in, their skills and talents. This not only makes residents feel more self-confident but makes the activity more relatable to others from that generation.

As they become more engaged, you will often find a resident who possesses such a strong knowledge or passion for the topic that, if supported by the rest of the group, can become the group's leader and can help plan and lead the activity. By encouraging residents to take more of a leadership role in the community's activity program, the Activity Director will have more free time to focus his or her talents elsewhere in further development of the program.

Perhaps one of the best programs for supporting resident independence is the Resident Ambassador Program. This is my favorite resident program. If you do not have one, I would highly recommend implementing one as soon as possible. In a lot of ways, moving into an LTC community is like transferring to a new high school and, whether excited or scared (or both), there is always an adjustment period.

The Resident Ambassador welcomes new residents into the community and serves as their mentor and a guide as they adjust to their new home and explore all the benefits your community has to offer. The Resident Ambassador will introduce them to the other residents, help them decide which activities they would enjoy the most, invite them to attend council meetings, and join them for their first few meals.

The residents working within this program have a sense of purpose and feel like an important part of the community. They have opportunity to help new residents get into routine and share the knowledge they have gained since moving into the community. By providing them a role, you are creating an environment for them to share their successes. This builds a person's self-esteem and empowers and encourages their engagement. The Resident Ambassador is not the only resident who benefits from the program. After moving into a community, new residents typically have a lot of questions. Instead of feeling like a "nuisance" because they are going to a member of management with new questions, they can reach out to a peer who remembers what it was like when they first arrived themselves.

I usually have two Resident Ambassadors, one male and one female. But you might want more, depending on the size of your community. I recommend selecting a resident who has been in the community for at least a few years, is respected and trusted by the other residents, is genuinely happy living there, and does not mind showing off their room (and has a room that presents well).

It has always been my motto that the best marketing a community can have is a happy resident. Based on this principle, I include a quick visit with the Resident Ambassador when providing a prospective resident with a tour of the community. This gives the prospective resident a chance to see what a room/apartment looks like when it is furnished and occupied. Around this time, I typically find an excuse to step away for a few minutes, allowing them a few minutes to talk alone. This gives the prospective resident an opportunity to ask "what the place is really like?" and a chance to "hear the truth" from someone who actually lives in the community, rather than employee who they might think is just telling them what they want to hear.

Although not a necessity, I like to give the Resident Ambassador a small plaque to hang outside their apartment to identify them as a Resident Ambassador. Not only does this help identify them to any new residents but it also shows appreciation for the important role they play. As an added bonus, it gives them something to show off to their family.

Because we are so focused on making sure our residents feel independent within our community, it might be easy to forget they are still part of the outside community. This is where they made an impact and important contributions, had jobs, hobbies, and relationships that were, and still are, a very important part of their lives. Protecting the independence of our residents means acknowledging the importance of their lives as part of the outside community. Helping them recognize that they are still an important part of their community and keeping them connected and engaged with that community should be a priority.

It is not only important to promote individuality and independence within your internal community, but also with the outside community. It is important for the outside community to know and understand what we do. They also need to have access to the information that is needed to make an informed decision about topics related to long-term care, it is our responsibility to provide that for them. I can help them walk through the process. I tell people that they can call me and ask questions anytime even in the case they do not chose my organization, it is about building the relationships. The outside community is a huge resource and referral source, they talk and if they have a positive experience with you, it is shared. It helps build the reputation in the community. The benefits would hopefully be increased census, improved reputations, building a network of referral sources, etc.

Anytime that you can combine a community event and an activity, you should. It is important for the residents to continue to feel a part of the community and it is important for the community to see that the residents are valued and treated as members of the community. Often the misconception is that once a person moves into long-term care, they are forgotten about, we want to promote that is not the case. Just because a person lives in long-term care, does not mean they stop living or that they are no longer a valued member of the community. The residents say a lot about the facility not only in what they say, but also in their appearance.

An example of this would be the important role that many residents have played as members of the American Community is the many veterans who served their country. By connecting them with other veterans in the outside community can stir strong feelings of importance in their lives and encourages great feeling of patriotism and a contribution to their country.

My very first community had about 10 veterans who served during peacetime or were active in WWII and Korea. To remind them of their importance to the outside community we had a new flag pole installed and had the local newspaper take a picture of our veterans in front of the new flag and put it on the front page thanking them for their service.

A former Assisted Living Director, and colleague of mine, acknowledged her veterans by arranging to have the American Legion come to her facility and dedicate an American flag and do a flag raising ceremony for the local community and it helped the residents to feel patriotic and reminisce about the pride they felt over their service.

Decorating and celebrating holidays in a big way can make residents feel acknowledged and special. Veteran's Decorate, have a special meal, and a decorated cake or other special dessert. During lunch on Mother's Day and Father's Day ask your residents to tell their funniest story about their kids. There are other days throughout the year that can be made special. How about aviation day or donut day?

I once worked in a community in a small rural town in Iowa where almost half of our residents were farmers and took great pride in their farm and the thousands of families that they helped feed. One of our nurses, who was also a farmer, helped remind them of their importance to the farming community by taking them to the county fair to see the livestock and talk about their farming days.

EMPLOYEE INDEPENDENCE

The first step in promoting independence with staff is to provide a robust and comprehensive orientation and training program. Begin with clearly explaining their job description and your expectations to ensure they are up to the task. Offer and encourage opportunities for continued development within the organization. The more a new employee feels invested in a company and their ability to "climb the ranks" the more they will seek to master their position. They will strive to be rewarded opportunities for advancement. One of the best feelings as an LTC administrator is watching a new hire move on to bigger and better things, knowing you had a part in their professional development.

Peer training is a great method of promoting independence with employees during the training process. Peer training is a necessary part of training. As managers, we should know the ins and outs of the department and its overarching goals, policies, and procedures, but no one knows it better than the employee doing the job, 40 hours (or more) a week. Showing employees that you trust them as a trainer gives them a sense of pride and allows them the ability to train the employee that they themselves would want to work with. However, it is very important that the trainer is knowledgeable, efficient, and able to devote the time and energy to the trainee for the new employee to be successful.

The second step in promoting independence with staff is to ensure information availability. An employee can only provide care as accurate as the information that they have. This means making sure all employees have access to the Electronic Medical Records (EMR) that they need. Many new CNAs, and even nurses, go days without having a login for the EMR. They must rely solely on second-hand information passed down from supervisors or coworkers. Always make sure that before an employee starts on the floor, they have all the logins they need to readily access any information, so that they can have the independence to have knowledge at their fingertips. Without which, your new employee will fundamentally feel decreased independence and self-sufficiency.

Another means to boost the availability of information for employees is to provide cheat sheets and At a Glance care plans. Rather than having to log in to the EMR and look up resident information, have this information printed (and up to date) at the nurses' station or another designated location. Some examples include a list of residents that are a fall risk and their fall interventions, a list of residents who need assistance with transfers, and if they are a 1 or 2 assist or use a mechanical lift, and a list of residents with oxygen and their concentrator settings. Another tool I have seen used with great success is laminated cards that contain items to be verified, such as oxygen settings, fall interventions, call lights in place, etc. When surveyors show up, the CNA's can quickly grab their "Survey Card" and check all their assigned rooms to make sure that everything is in place.

Ensuring our employees have all the information they need to do their job safely and efficiently, will result in an increase in employee initiative as they will have the confidence and self-esteem to carry out their duties independently. With this, you will see a decrease in the need to micromanage.
In addition to making sure our employees have access to all the information they need to be independent care givers, it is equally important to make sure they have access to all the tools they need to do their job independently.

This includes ensuring all equipment, such as mechanical lifts and dietary appliances, are fully operational and that all supply rooms, resident rooms, and pantries are stocked with all essential materials. There is very little more frustrating for a caregiver than to be in the middle of caring for a resident only to realize that they do not have what they need to complete the task and now must stop the process, remove their PPE, wash up, locate the resources needed to finish the task, required PPE back on, and resume where they left off.

This is frustrating for both the employee, who is now (further) behind schedule and the resident, who now must wait to have their needs attended to. Besides being frustrating for the employee, scenarios such as the previous example also have a financial component. Because the employee is now unable to take their break or must stay late to finish everything before shift change payroll expenses will go up. Also, the employee may be so focused on getting what they need quickly to finish caring for their resident, they may "borrow" supplies from another resident's room or just grab what they need from the supply room without properly signing them out for proper billing and reimbursement or, worse, having another resident pay for supplies they did not use.

Every day you should be rounding the community and meeting with staff to verify that all supply areas are stocked and that all equipment is in its assigned location. Ensure staff do not have to go searching for what they need. Make sure that all equipment is on a preventative maintenance schedule, and periodically audit for compliance and minimize the likelihood of unexpected equipment failure. Imagine having a resident mid-transfer on a mechanical lift and it suddenly fails. Be prepared when equipment failure does occur. These machines need repaired or replaced as soon as possible so that employees are not having to share equipment. Sharing equipment takes twice as long to deliver care and encourages staff to engage in unsafe practices to save time. An example (which I myself am guilty of) would be transferring a resident without using a lift when one is required per their plan of care. This can be dangerous for both the employee and the resident and could potentially put the organization in a precarious situation.

By guaranteeing your employees have access to all the tools and information they would require, you have taken the next step in promoting their independence. By ensuring availability of resources and materials, employees will be able to go about their day as independently and efficiently as possible. Now that you have done your part in ensuring employees have all the resources, they require it is up to them to take the initiative to be as independent and proficient as possible.

It is also important to promote independence with staff by encouraging them to provide their input and ideas. Something simple like allowing employees an opportunity to vote on what color you paint the break room, or what the theme of the next community party is lets them know that they are a valued member of the team and that their voice and opinion is important and matters. Make sure you are having regular in-services and present issues to the employees who do the job every day and solicit their input in coming up with a solution. Daily or weekly huddles with your staff is another great way to communicate your needs and to hear their needs or concerns.

For those employees who are perhaps too shy to speak up in group setting, make sure you are rounding the community often and checking in with employees privately to allow them a chance to offer their input, concerns, or frustrations.

Always have an open-door policy so that employees can come to you with ideas and concerns. Also, make it known that they can come to you to voice any concerns without fear of repercussions. I jokingly tell employees that along with an open-door policy I also have a "closed-door policy," in which they can come to me with any concerns, even if it is directed at me, or to tell me I am wrong, without fear of retaliation. In exchange, I request that it is behind closed doors and not in front of family, staff, or residents. But you have to actually mean this and be prepared to hear things that you don't want to (but might need to) hear.

Another great way to encourage employee input is in the scheduling process. By offering flexible schedules to employees and allowing them a choice in what days or shifts they work, they are empowered to take ownership and accountability of their schedule (Howington, 2020). This makes them feel valued and like their outside lives matter.

By giving them flexibility in their schedules, you reduce the likelihood of call-ins. You are also likely to see less turnover. Employees will be less likely to go somewhere else that would offer hours that better accommodate their outside life. Some managers will even take it as far as letting the employees fill out their own schedule with the understanding that it will be reviewed and may be adjusted for any overtime reductions, or to ensure adequate coverage.

By allowing employees to provide input in their workplace you will promote a culture where they will feel valued and appreciated. They will begin to see their role as an important participant in pushing forward the team's efforts to build a community. A community that provides the highest quality of care imaginable for your residents as well as a fun and empowering place to work. Your staff will continue growing in their role, will become increasingly independent and trustworthy, and will require very little oversight.

Unfortunately, as employees become more independent and require less oversight, many managers make the fatal error of shifting their focus on newer employees or employees who might require more oversight due to performance concerns. Although it is important to provide support to new or struggling employees, do not slack on your commitment to those who have already demonstrated their contributions, and ability to work independently. Once an employee reaches this level of independence, it is most important to be an attentive and effective leader and encourage and empower the employee in being as independent as they can be.

The final step in promoting independence with staff is to continuously reinforce and guide them in enhancing their critical thinking and problem-solving skills. You should still be meeting with the employee regularly and having honest discussions about any struggles or challenges they might be facing. As leaders, it is in our nature to try to provide an answer or solution to any issue or challenge that we are presented with. Although tempting, and often what the employee is looking for, this will not benefit them in the long run. As a leader and mentor, it is your duty to inspire the employee to become a confidant, capable, and independent problem solver.

I came up with the acronym E.L.F., to remind myself of this:

Encourage employees to find their own solutions,
Let them fail from time to time,
Forgive Mistakes.

Although you need to help the employee in addressing any challenges they might be having, do not provide answers or solutions right away, even if you have one. Encourage them to come up with their own solution. Just like anything else, critical thinking and problem solving takes practice. Start by asking them questions and letting them come up with an answer on their own. Try beginning the conversation with, "So what would you do if you were the administrator?" By framing the question this way, you let the employee know that you value their experiences and opinions and believe they are capable of rationalizing and problem solving on their own.

There will most certainly be times when you will think the employee is making a mistake or is not making the best decision. If you believe the employee is making a mistake or not taking something into consideration, provide them your rationale and have a discussion. If they still feel like their proposition is the better solution, and you know the outcome will result in no real detriment, let the employee make the call. Let them know the logic behind why you disagree but that you will support their decision, and if it ends up being a mistake will work through it together. Make sure the employee knows that this is not a false platitude and that this will be a learning experience for both of you. No one wants to take a risk or make a decision that will lead to some form of disciplinary action or reprisal.

Although a learning experience, this can be a great exercise in promoting critical thinking skills. Make sure you are exercising increased oversight and attention to detail to ensure there are no negative consequences to the residents or the organization *and* be prepared to help the employee deal with the fallout in a non-judgmental and educational manner, if indeed the outcome is negative. Sometime situations can pleasantly surprise us.

If the decision does turn out to be a mistake, remind them that this was a learning experience and that mistakes are expected, tolerated, and forgiven. Talk through the situation and guide them in formulating a solution and what they think should be done differently in the future. If you are thoughtful and supportive, the employee will appreciate your guidance and will be motivated to try again. Allowing an employee to make their own mistake will help them learn and grow to make better decisions in the future.

Conversely, the employee might see the problem from a different perspective than you do and come up with a better option than the one you would have proposed, and you will have learned something from them. As I mentioned in a previous section, there are many ways to complete the same tasks. If you employ this method of developing independence with employees consistently, this *will* happen. When it does, make sure to praise the employee for their problem-solving skills and reward them in some way. Again, a hand-written letter goes a long way.

3
HEALTH & SAFETY

Because I work in the healthcare industry, it is no surprise that I have 'health' as a fundamental core value for success. After all, it's in the name. Before joining our communities, many residents have already made the difficult decision to sell the homes, where countless cherished family memories were formed as well as many of the possessions that they have worked their entire lives for. They move, not because they *want* to but because they *need* to. They now depend on us to provide them the extra needed care and to respond, not only in addressing declines in health, but also to proactively prevent these declines.

As healthcare professionals, we have a legal (and moral) obligation in helping and supporting our residents in being as healthy as they choose - and is reasonably possible. In so doing, the resident will typically be better able to care for themselves and will retain a more positive outlook. Not only is this what we want for our residents, but it also results in a reduced workload for your staff and fewer complaints to the State or Ombudsman.

Health is not only a fundamental core value with respect to our residents but also for our staff. Healthier employees tend to be more productive, call in less, and generally have a more positive personality. This helps promote a more efficient workplace and enhances employee engagement and staff morale. As a result of a healthy staff, you will enjoy lower turnover, a reduction in employee conflicts and complaints, and overall better care provided to your residents. Healthier employees are also less likely to suffer from caregiver burnout, which is one the biggest contributing factor in resident abuse. Essentially, 'health" refers to being free from a disease or illness that may cause harm.

While this is important, there are also many potentially harmful accidental and external events that we need to consider when safeguarding the well-being of our staff and residents. These include natural threats such as tornados or floods, electrical shocks or fires, and workplace injuries, just to name a few. Being protected from external accidents and undesired events is referred to as 'Safety.'

Initially, there were to be four core values with health and safety each being a separate core value. However, as I continued to examine how much health and safety impact one another, I realized that they were so interconnected that they could essentially be viewed as a shared core value.

By taking the steps outlined in this section, you will see a reduction in workplace accidents which will not only benefit your staff by keeping them safe from injury but also see an increase savings in associated worker's compensation costs. This will result in a higher quality of care for our residents and better survey outcomes.

RESIDENT HEALTH & SAFETY

As healthcare providers, we are entrusted with providing the highest quality of healthcare services. This includes addressing any current health issues your residents are experiencing but also protecting them from health problems that are preventable or minimizing all possible risk factors. According to CMS:
Quality of care is a fundamental principle that applies to all treatment and care provided to facility residents...(and) the facility must ensure that residents receive treatment and care in accordance with professional standards of practice... (Quality of care, 2019).

Healthcare Hack

Personally pass the snack cart a few random days and make a mental note of residents who consistently decline.

Go back and casually visit with the residents who did not take a snack and find out their reasons and what you can do to provide them with a snack they would enjoy.

An important aspect of any healthy lifestyle is to ensure proper hydration and nutrition standards are being followed. Nutrition is the main goal of menu programs. Although sometimes necessary, specialized diets should be kept to a minimum because they are often too restrictive, and people just quit eating. Older people many times cannot taste much, but sweets are something they can usually still taste and enjoy. The first thing a diabetic diet does is take away sweets. Instead, work with your dietitian on the frequency and portion size of sweets offered instead of complete elimination. Liberalized diets should be used as often as possible, not just as a matter of promoting calorie consumption but to promote independence. No one wants to be told what they can and cannot eat, and if they are (or perceive they are) many will simply quit eating and have undesired weight loss. When this occurs, residents are often given supplements. Supplements are costly and not as enjoyable for the resident.

Providing healthy snacks between meals is another way we promote the health of our residents. It is important especially if you have weight loss in your building. It should have high quality nutritional choices. But we all know "junk food" is still a preferred choice, and a fun choice. However, sometimes any calories are better than no calories at all. The trick is to make sure they get offered.

Meals and drinks need to be served in accordance with doctors' orders to avoid safety concerns such as choking or aspirating. Some communities utilize alternating meal managers to observe the dining experience and ensure diets are being followed, but I prefer an "all hands-on deck" approach, with all available management helping.

> # Healthcare Hack
>
> Get management involved in meal pass!
>
> This can be done by assigning different days to each manager, or you can take a more laissez-faire approach and take it day by day.
>
> There should always be at least two managers helping serve.

Whichever you choose, make sure that meals are being frequently audited to ensure diets are being followed, meals and drinks are served at the proper temperature, and staff are using correct food handling procedures. This is exactly what surveyors will do when they visit, so make sure staff are in the habit of being watched

A strong Infection Control Program with a designated Infection Control Nurse is required to ensure we are protecting residents from communicable diseases common in long-term care; MRSA, CDIF, and UTIs from indwelling catheters or improper peri care are among the most common in LTC settings.

An Infection Control Program should continuously monitor resident infections, audit infection control policy and perdure compliance, and provide ongoing training and education for staff.

According to CMS:

> All SNFs must have a designated infection
> preventionist whom works at least part time and is
> responsible for the Infection Control Program.
> This employee must have professional training in
> nursing, medical technology, microbiology,
> epidemiology, or another related field. They must
> also have completed specialized training in
> infection prevention and control (Infection Control,
> 2019).

Typically, this person would be responsible for tracking antibiotics
and infections, ensuring antibiotics are appropriate for the infection,
tracking and trending infections within the community, and
identifying any possible root causes which need to be addressed
through QAPI. Utilize your Infection Control Officer to include
monthly infection control tips in your community newsletter and
cover infection control topics and education at your monthly In-
service.

The infection preventionist should also ensure proper staff
education on infection control procedure, to prevent the spread of
infectious diseases such as MRSA, VRE, CDIFF, Influenza, and the
Norovirus. This would include hand
washing, proper PPE usage, and
proper linen and garbage disposal.
A strong Infection Control Program
would also cover proper peri-care
training and audits to ensure staff
are providing in care accordance
with professional standards to
prevent UTIs and skin breakdowns,
which can lead to pressure ulcers
and potential infection.

Healthcare Hack

Attach mesh bags that
containing disinfectant
wipes to all lifts.   This will
allow staff to easily and
quickly disinfect equipment
after each use.

Proper catheter and ostomy care should also be a focus as they
are a host to all sorts of bacteria. Being clean and odor free is not
only a requirement of an Infection Control Program, but also a

necessity in protecting dignity and self-esteem, which promote mental health.

Minimizing cross contamination is a key aspect of any Infection Control Program. Disinfecting equipment after every use to avoid cross contamination is important and should be documented.

Another way to prevent cross contamination among residents is by minimizing shared supplies. To accomplish this, you need to ensure an adequate inventory of supplies. Each resident should be assigned their own glucometers, transfer slings, gait belts, or any other frequently used items.

In addition to providing our residents with exemplary healthcare services, it is also important to protect them from any accidental injuries that might have a negative impact on their quality of life.

According to CMS:

> The facility must ensure that the resident environment remains as free of accident hazards as is possible (and) each resident receives adequate supervision and assistance devices to prevent accidents (Accidents, 2019).

Healthcare Hack

Ensure that all assistive devices are on a preventative maintenance schedule to ensure that they are in in working order and that there is sufficient documentation that every effort is being made to prevent injuries due to faulty equipment.

This includes environmental issues, such as water on the floor, clutter, unsecured chemicals, or faulty equipment. If a resident requires the use of an assistive device to minimize the risk of accident, the facility is responsible to ensure that the resident is provided adequate training, proper oversight, and that the devices are in working order for them.

Accidents resulting in harm to the resident involve reporting to the State and completing an internal investigation into the root cause of the accident. Preventative measures must also be documented.

Accidents not resulting in harm still require interventions be put into place to minimize the likelihood that an accident will reoccur. When establishing an intervention, it is important to develop a method to consistently monitor that these interventions are being followed.

A "Falling Star" program can help with fall reduction. Fall Risks can be identified by placing an identifier, such as a magnet or sticker, outside of resident's rooms. It cannot be obvious what this identifier means to ensure you are respecting the resident's privacy and remaining HIPAA compliant.

Another tool you can use to increase communication would be to provide employees with a folder or book at each nurses' station that lists interventions that are in place for each resident. At a minimum, this should be checked at the beginning and end of the shift, or whenever a resident becomes restless or agitated.

Healthcare Hack

Implement a binder at each Nurses Station that identifies residents on the unit who are a fall risk and summarize what their fall interventions are.

This should be checked immediately upon entrance of surveyors so that if an intervention is not in place, it is discovered and corrected by community staff instead of surveyors who could then issue a deficiency. Fall interventions should also be checked by managers during daily QA Rounds.

To prevent falls from improper transfers, especially for new or agency staff, create transfer cards that identifies whether a resident is a one or two assist, or if they require the use of a mechanical lift and what type of lift should be used. Again, these should be maintained in a private area in the resident's room to ensure HIPPA compliance. You need to have a designated person responsible for updating these to ensure they are always up to date. It does no good, and is counterproductive, to have these available to staff with incorrect or outdated information.

These methods can be very beneficial to residents and staff if implemented appropriately. But you need to have systems in place to ensure information is accurate and up to date at all times. You must also guarantee that this information is only available or identifiable to nursing staff to safeguard the privacy and dignity of the resident.

The overall effectiveness of the community's ability to promote health and safety within the community is measured through QAPI. A strong and meaningful QAPI program is one that is individualized by using the facility assessment. You must know your weak areas and be able to prioritize according to what is most critical. The department heads need to be on board with this and be engaged in your QAPI's PIP teams. You get better buy-in from the staff if they are included in the process and can see the progress.

Progress should be posted for all staff to see. In some cases, the residents and family should also have access to the data, good or bad, so everyone knows what you are working on, if it is working, or if you need to tweak your program. Look at health concerns affecting residents such as wounds, UTIs, flu rates, catheters, anti-psychotics, and appropriate diagnoses. Look at resident safety concerns such as falls, type of fall, fall interventions, and appropriate assistive devices. Injuries, resident-to-resident abuse, elder abuse, and any notable cognitive declines that might put a resident's safety at risk.

One of the best methods in monitoring and ensuring that health and safety standards are being adhered to is by implementing a QA Rounding program. No one person can ensure that every health and safety measure is in place. But through divide and concur, your team can ensure that basic standards are being met. All members of the facility leadership team should be assigned designated rooms which they are responsible for visiting and inspecting daily. Develop a QA checklist of items to be monitored that can be used to document any concerns and note any trends.

Your QA checklist needs to be facility specific and continuously evolving based on areas of improvement identified through QAPI. At a minimum, your QA Rounds should include basic health and safety expectations, including compliance with the Life Safety Code, ensuring fall interventions are in place, call lights are in place, and inspecting the room for any noticeable maintenance concerns or safety hazards. QA Rounds should include a brief visit with the resident to discuss any concerns they might have, monitoring for signs of abuse, and being vigilant of any signs of distress or notable changes.

By protecting the health and safety of our residents, you will strengthen the first two core values by enhancing independence and defending dignity. By creating a community that protects the health and safety of your residents you will see an overall increase in resident satisfaction and quality of life. In turn, you will enjoy a decrease in hospitalization and an improvement in quality measures. Both of which positively affect your reimbursement.

EMPLOYEE HEALTH & SAFETY

In 2018, work-related deaths and injuries in the United States were estimated to cost about $170 billion dollars (National Safety Council, 2020). To put this into perspective, this is about 24% of total US military spending that same year (Robert Burns, 2018). According to the U.S. Bureau of Labor Statistics, the healthcare industry ranked among the highest for nonfatal occupational injuries and illnesses in the private industry sector in 2017 (U.S. Bureau of Labor Statistics, 2020). It is because of these high rates of employee work-place injuries (including my own back issues) that leads me to include safety among my top core values.

Employee protections are protected by OSHA, which requires:

> Each employer shall furnish to each of his employees' employment and a place of employment which are free from recognized hazards that are causing or are likely to cause death or serious physical harm to his employees (Duties of Employers and Employees, 2018).

OSHA is extremely important for the health and safety of employees. An OSHA inspection forces a facility to look at safety practices it may not normally look at, including blood borne pathogens, right to know laws, physical equipment inspections, etc.

When it comes to employee safety, being proactive is key. The best way to proactively address workplace safety with your employees is through a strong training and orientation. A strong safety training and orientation program covers all aspects of employee safety and accident prevention. Safety Orientation should be unique to the community and individualized for each position. Safety Orientation should be covered with all new hires, before they are even allowed to set foot on the floor. It is always great to include all department heads in new hire safety orientation to cover safety items as they relate to each department.

Things that often get missed are emergency shut offs for the building and dietary rules/regulations for staff not working in the kitchen. As the old saying goes, "safety is everyone's responsibility," and it requires dedicated staff who do things the right way and don't take shortcuts. You can encourage and support your staff in their dedication and commitment to safety by not just covering workplace safety in orientation, but continuously reviewing and returning to the topics thereafter.

Healthcare Hack

Give an honest assessment of your community's Safety Committee and identify 5 things you can do to improve it and make an action plan.

If you need assistance with this, you can reach out to your State's Health Care Association and they can connect you with someone who can help. Additionally, feel free to contact me.

The best way to provide ongoing training and support to your staff is through the community's safety committee. As an AIT, I studied under an administrator who had served on the board of directors of a worker's compensation insurance company. He shared with me his first-hand account of the savings associated with worker's compensation insurance and lost time claims experienced by communities that placed a high priority on their safety committee versus those that did not.

During his tutelage, this administrator emphasized the important role the safety committee plays in reducing costs, providing a safe and secure work environment, and promoting staff morale by demonstrating your commitment to keeping them safe. He encouraged me to share in his passion and commitment to the Safety Committee and prepared me to do so by sharing much of his knowledge and advice; some of which I will now share with you. A strong and effective Safety Committee is one that is active within the community, meets regularly (at least monthly), and involves management, front line staff, and sometimes even residents or families. The Safety Committee should continuously review (and revise) systems and procedures, conduct regular audits, and set clear goals and objectives. This information should be documented in your monthly minutes and communicated to all stakeholders in the community.

The Safety Committee needs to be an integral part of QAPI. Safety Committee minutes should be reviewed during your QAPI Meeting and its members should be actively involved in the performance improvement process, including ongoing staff training and education.

Another way to encourage and support worker safety is through a safety incentive program which rewards employees for their commitment to safety. These rewards can be given when reaching certain milestones, such as days without injury or days without lost time. A 2001 study showed that companies that implemented a safety incentive program experienced an average 44% decline in lost-time injuries compared to companies that did not (Goodrum & Gangwar, 2010). These incentives come in many forms such as monetary rewards, gifts, or even PTO.

If you currently do not have an employee safety incentive program and decide it would be beneficial for your community to implement one, get creative and have fun with and it. Most importantly, visit with staff and find out what sort of program they would find motivating and what kind of incentives would they like to see. Once you have built a program, train all staff and ensure they understand how the program works and what its purpose is. Make sure to stress that the program is to reward workplace safety and not to discourage accident reporting.

Another benefit that can be provided to staff that will promote workplace safety is a shoe allowance. Provide this to new employees upon hire and annually thereafter. In 2018, 26% of non-fatal, workplace injuries that resulted in lost time were due to slips trips and falls (U.S. Bureau of Labor Statistics, 2020). Improper or worn-out footwear can be a contributing factor in slips, trips, and fall. By providing an allowance for this, you can require proper footwear be worn by all employees without putting those who are struggling financially at a disadvantage. It also shows appreciation for employees who are constantly on their feet.

Now that we have kept our staff safe and accident free, let's look at ways we can keep them healthy as well. Encouraging healthier staff increases efficiency, reduces call-ins, and generally results in happier employees that are more engaged and make the community an overall more pleasant place for our residents to live. According to an article in Personnel Today, the average annual absentee rate for employee illnesses is 4.4 days per worker (Webber, 2019). For a community with 50 employees this equates to 220 shifts per year. For a larger facility with 100 employees, you are looking at 440 shifts per year. These would either go unfilled or would result in overtime or pickup bonuses.

Although tempting, avoid calling on the guy who always says yes because he will wear himself sick. If this employee becomes worn out and their health deteriorates, not only are they unable to pick up shifts but additionally they start calling in themselves, worsening the situation. He will also begin to feel used, unappreciated, and as if he is being punished for being a good employee. As managers, you need to be aware of this and intervene before burnout or health issues set in.

Healthcare Hack

Implement an Employee Health and Wellness Program

Benefits of healthy staff include improved cognition resulting in better decision making and more accurate charting. You will also see an increase in productivity which will result in quicker call light response time, higher quality of care, and less tasks being carried over from one shift to the next. You are also likely to see improved morale which will result in less call-ins and fewer workplace injuries.

One way to demonstrate that employee health is a priority is by implementing an Employee Health Program. You can accomplish this by appointing a Health and Wellness Ambassador to lead this program. This can be a Nurse, CNA, or other employee with a passion for personal health. The Health and Wellness Ambassador would work with the DON, LNHA, and Employee Engagement Committee to brainstorm ideas and assist with planning.

The Health and Wellness Ambassador would be responsible for sending out a monthly health awareness email that provides tips for healthy living, educational videos and articles, and even have a dedicated section in the monthly newsletter. The Health and Wellness Ambassador would be a great resource to provide employees with connections to outside health groups such as counseling/therapists, yoga, martial arts, national and weight management, hiking trails, cycling groups, spiritual groups, and smoking cessation programs, just to name a few.

Part of this program would include coordinating team building events that promote health and wellness such as 5K walks, polar plunges, and company sports teams. You can also engage some healthy (pun intended) health competitions such as Biggest Loser and Fit Bit Competitions for your more competitive employees.

Another project that can be delegated to your Health and Wellness Ambassador is to create a calm and relaxing break or meditation room for employees to unwind and de-stress on their breaks, or to offer healthier snack options instead of the traditional unhealthy options you will often find from the vending machine, which often leaves staff feeling lethargic.

Depending on available funds, you can also host guest presenters like reflexologists, motivational speakers, or have a message therapist visit. Offering free (or discounted) gym memberships is another great tool to promote employee wellness and is a great fringe benefit that can be used in employee recruitment.

Promoting a workplace that emphasizes employee health will increase employee efficiency and productivity, resulting in the delivery of a higher quality of care to our residents. By improving the overall health of your staff, you will see a reduction in absenteeism and turnover. This will reduce the burden of staffing shortages and the associated negative impact on resident care.

CONCLUSION

Nursing homes have a reputation for being lonely, depressing, and institutional feeling. This contrasts with the desirable homey and community-based settings that most strive to mimic. Community is about coming together, residents and staff, for a common cause. The goal is to co-regulate consistent success and comfort. Building this unity between residents and staff directly correlates to pride, consistency, and a solid standard of care. As the relationship grows between them, there will be an increased familiarity with client preferences and an improvement in the care provided. Having a symbiotic give-and-take like this promotes an environment in which residents and staff thrive. The residents know their needs and wants are being recognized, and the staff are empowered to continue with genuine and exemplary care.

Transmuting intentions to these three Core Values is the first step in transforming your facility into a community. Happy residents result in fewer grievances, positive word of mouth, and better survey outcomes. Happy staff will result in reduced costs with staffing needs, decreased overtime and agency expenses, and a higher quality of care given and received.

As we have examined, dignity is a desire shared by all people. To treat someone with dignity is to respect their opinions and values and recognize that that their desires are equal to your own. When promoting dignity among the staff, you will cultivate a sense of loyalty to you, the organization, and the residents. Dignity must be exercised by every employee at every level of the organization so that it bleeds through into every level of care. Follow the Golden Rule, treat staff the way you would want to be treated, and empower them to treat the residents the way they would want to be treated.

Independence helps increase self-value and self-esteem, which directly impacts not only mental well-being, but physical as well. The most important thing you can do to protect resident independence is ensuring staff receive the proper education and training. Employees feel a sense of respect and trust when their employer gives them independence in their job. Promoting independence with both residents and staff will empower both your residents and staff to achieve and sustain their highest potential.

Finally, protecting and promoting the health and safety of our residents and staff will strengthen and supplement our first two core values by enhancing independence and protecting dignity. By creating a community that protects the health and safety of your staff and residents you will see an overall increase in resident satisfaction and quality of life and your employees will be more productive, call in less, and you will positively influence employee engagement and staff morale. As a result of this you reduce caregiver burnout and the likelihood of resident abuse.

These core values have guided me in my mission to destroy the stereotype that nursing homes are cold and institutional, like the facility where I would visit Jeanette as a child. I welcome you to join me in my mission of transforming the lives of our residents and caregivers by cultivating communities in which our residents thrive, and our caregivers are engaged and empowered. One facility at a time.

Remember Your Passion!

Healthcare Hack

My final piece of advice is to remember your passion. Remember why you chose this career in the first place.

It can be especially helpful to keep a small memento that reminds you of this on your desk or in your office. You can be having a bad day, but when you see this token, it will remind you of your passion. Suddenly you will find yourself focusing on the good.

I keep a picture on my desk of me and a resident taken before prom over 15 years ago.

Anthony Brewer began his career in healthcare as a Dietary Assistant before he was old enough to drive. He continued as a CNA while he worked his way through high school, college, and graduate school. His bottom-to-top experience in his field, passion for servant leadership, and understanding of both the human and administrative aspects of healthcare give him a truly unique perspective.

With over twenty years of knowledge and experience in healthcare, Anthony has a proven track record of success in creating real culture change by focusing on providing dignity, independence, and health & safety to his residents and staff. Brewer is committed to transforming facilities into communites by nurturing professional development and impacting the lives of residents and their families.

A. Brewer
MPA LNHA HSE

- ✓ Certified Dementia Units
- ✓ Privately Owned
- ✓ Assisted Living
- ✓ Skilled Nursing
- ✓ Home Health Care
- ✓ Corporations
- ✓ Non-Profits
- ✓ Faith-Based
- ✓ Rural Markets
- ✓ Urban Markets

REFERENCES

Accidents, 42 C.F.R. § 483.35 (2019).

Activities, 42 C.F.R. § 483.25(c)(1) (2019).

Comprehensive person centered-care plan, 42 C.F.R. § 483.21 (2019).

Duties of employers and employees, 29 U.S.C. § 654 (2019).

Goodrum, Paul & Gangwar, Manish. (2010). Safety Incentives A study of their effectiveness in construction. Professional Safety. 49. (Goodrum, 2010).

Grievances, 42 C.F.R. § 483.10(j)(4) (2019).

Howington, J. (2020, August 20). How Flexible Work Benefits Companies and Employees. [Blog post]. Retrieved from https://www.flexjobs.com/employer-blog/the-benefits-of-allowing-employees-a-flexible-schedule/.

Infection control, 42 C.F.R. § 483.80 (2019).

Judge, T. A., Piccolo, R. F., Podsakoff, N. P., Shaw, J. C., & Rich, B. L. (2010, October 01). The relationship between pay and job satisfaction: A meta-analysis of the literature. *Journal of Vocational Behavior*, 77(2), 157-167. https://doi.org/10.1016/j.jvb.2010.04.002.

Merriam-Webster. *Dignity*. Merriam-Webster. https://www.merriamwebster.com/dictionary/dignity#:~:text =1%20%3A%20the%20quality%20or%20state,from%20M erriam%2DWebster%20on%20dignity.

Mobility, 42 C.F.R. § 483.25(c)(3) (2019).

National Safety Council. (2020, February 20). *Work Injury Costs*. Injury Facts. https://injuryfacts.nsc.org/work/costs/work-injury-costs/.

Privacy and Confidentiality, 42 C.F.R. § 483.10(h)(1) (2019).

Quality of care, 42 C.F.R. § 483.10 (2019).

Resident rights, 42 C.F.R. § 483.10(a)(1) (2019).

Robert Burns, R. L. (2018, February 11). *A Pentagon Budget Like None Before: $700 Billion*. Military.com. https://www.military.com/daily-news/2018/02/11/pentagon-budget-none-700-billion.html.

Self-determination, 42 C.F.R. § 483.10(f)(2019).

U.S. Bureau of Labor Statistics, (2020, November 04). Injuries, Illnesses, and Fatalities. Retrieved October 26, 2020, from https://www.bls.gov/iif/oshwc/osh/case/cd_r1_2019.htm.

Webber, A. (2019, November 6). *Sickness absence increases to 4.4 days per worker*. Personnel Today. https://www.personneltoday.com/hr/sickness-absence-2018-increase/.